Simple. Delicious.
And
Very French

Yolande Favreau
Lisa Dane

Design: Lucie Favreau
Final Layout: Jessica Grimault

For the next generation of chefs

Lucie, Nina, Mathieu, Alice
&
Nora and William "Mac"

A Note from Yolande Favreau
Author & Chef de Cuisine

Cooking has always been a passion for me-a kind of creativity. I took several classes with well-known chefs in Paris and spent countless hours in the kitchen trying recipes until the result was perfect. Now I offer you my simplified French recipes.

My husband Jean-Claude and I spent several years in many countries where we appreciated different cultures and cuisines. We spent four years in the U.S. and it was during this time that I met my friend Lisa. We both belonged to a warm and very friendly international organization. Lisa and I shared many of the same passions: Reading, art, French culture and gourmet cuisine.

A few years ago, Jean-Claude and I moved back to Paris. One day my dear friend Lisa asked me, "What if we were to create a cookbook together? A very simple book that does not intimidate those who love French cuisine?"

The idea germinated very gradually in my head. Using only a few ingredients is difficult for me because most of my recipes include a dozen ingredients or more. But I love my friend Lisa and I really wanted to rise to the challenge.

I didn't realize that authoring a cookbook would be so much investment in time and sometimes I was discouraged. But one day my grand-daughter Lucie (who is studying design at university) offered to design the cookbook. I was delighted because Lucie and I had shared many "gourmet moments" cooking together in my kitchen.

This cookbook contains delicious recipes that are quick to prepare. Most are gluten-free and lactose-free. These recipes are perfect for people who have busy lives and don't have a lot of time to spend in the kitchen. You, your family and your friends will love the results.

Don't be afraid to try these recipes…you are going to love them!

A Note from Lisa Dane
Editor

I don't cook. I mean I REALLY do not cook. Long ago, a friend sewed me an apron with the words, "I'd Rather Eat than Cook". True then and true now.

But with good luck and by happenstance, I met a wonderful Parisian in our Indianapolis organization, the Association of International Women. Yolande Favreau opened up my eyes, ears and taste buds as she tutored refresher French to our select, small conversation group. Our class syllabus expanded to include elements of French culture and cuisine. It wasn't long before we enthusiastically enhanced our language and writing composition skills by including champignon (mushroom) sampling. Grammatical accent marks were palatable as we swooned over pommes de terre gratinée (scalloped potatoes with cheese sauce). We sipped champagne while learning the correct placement of a cédille.

Yolande and her husband Jean-Claude eventually moved back to their large, quintessentially Haussmann-style Paris apartment. We've remained friends over the years... and I am stll not an assured cook.

Watching Yolande swiftly and confidently create 4-course dinners and confections in her kitchen, I (as any American) was impressed and somewhat intimidated. «But no...it is easy!» Yolande asserts as she flies around her kitchen.

And so an idea was born. Could Yolande create a cookbook of EASY French recipes for the busy American Francophile without enough time, talent or training? A cookbook of recipes, each containing relatively few ingredients, taking minutes (rather than hours) to assemble? Never one to dodge a challenge, Yolande agreed to share some of her chef secrets. *Simple. Delicious. And Very French* is a cookbook full of recipes that are easy and, most importantly, authentically French.

Whenever I want or I need to prepare an appetizer, dinner, or dessert, ***Simple. Delicious. & Very French*** is my go-to. I love these recipes that fit a busy American lifestyle and still provide that certain «je ne sais quoi» élan of classic French cuisine. I simply roll up my sleeves; tie on an apron and ...Voila!

Introduction

Maybe you fell in love with Paris. A sunny morning people-watching at a café, you swooned over butter croissants and café crème for breakfast. Or a crisp salade Niçoise for lunch. Or a warm dish of Pot au Feu in a cozy bistro during a misty evening on the Seine.

But now you are back home. No time to cook. No French culinary skill. Julia Child? No way, s'il vous plait!

Your friends, or in-laws or co-workers are coming over. What to do? You want to wow them but you may not have time or cooking skills.

For Boomers who love France and French cuisine, for Millennials who have international tastes but not enough time to cook, for people who simply don't like to cook but need a few recipes to impress, **Simple. Delicious. And Very French** is for you.

Parisian Yolande Favreau has classical expertise, cooking and baking scrumptious meals and pastries that delight her family and friends. This cookbook is filled with easy, quick and delectable recipes using just a few ingredients but with plenty of French flair.

Who doesn't love a creamy, warm soup on a chilly day? You and your guests will swoon over **Velouté aux Champignons** (Creamy Mushroom Soup). Want the same tender deliciousness of **Boeuf Bourguignon** (Beef Burgundy) à la Julie & Julia without spending hours in your kitchen? And desserts like **Fondant Chocolat** (Molten Chocolate cakes), **Choux à la Crème and Eclairs au Chocolat** (Cream Puffs and Chocolate Eclairs) and classic **Madeleines**? Ooh, la la! With simple, step-by-step directions, **Simple. Delicious. And Very French** will help a non-cook, non-chef, non-expert do this!

Bon appétit!

Sommaire
Contents

🍼 = Lactose-free

🌾 = Gluten-free

Amuses-Bouche
Appetite Prelude

Gougères Cheese Puffs	12
Sablés au Parmiggiano Cocktail Cheese Crackers	13
Pissaladière French Pissaladiere	14
🍼 *Rillettes de Sardines* Smoked Sardine Canapes	15
🌾 *Gaspacho de Betterave* Beetroot Gazpacho	16

Entrées
Appetizers

🍼🌾 *Salade Niçoise* Salad Nicoise	20
Quiche Lorraine Quiche Lorraine	21
🌾 *Omelette aux Fines Herbes* Herbed Omelet	22
🌾 *Soupe à l'Oignon* French Onion Soup	23
🌾 *Velouté aux Champignons* Creamy Mushroom Soup	24

Plats Principaux
Main Courses

🌾 *Sole Meunière* Classic Sole Meuniere	28
🌾 *Saumon avec Riz Pilaf* Crispy Salmon with Rice Pilaf	29
🌾 *Boeuf Bourguignon* Beef Burgundy	30
🍼 🌾 *Pot au Feu* Beef Brisket with Vegetables	31
🌾 *Parmentier de Canard* Duck and Potato Casserole	32
🌾 *Purée de Pomme de Terre* French Potato Puree	33

Desserts

Crème Brûlée	Classic Crème Brûlée	36
Fondant Chocolat	Molten Chocolat Cake	37
Choux à la Crème	Cream Puff Pastry	38
L'Île Flottante	Floating Island	39
Pavlova	Pavlova Berry Meringue	40

L'Heure du Thé
Teatime Treats

Madeleines Chocolat	Chocolate Madeleines	44
Financiers	French Financier Cakes	45
Quatre Quart	Fluted Mini Pound Cakes	46
Les Gâteaux de Maman	Mama's Little Cakes	47
Sablés Diamant	Diamond Butter Cookies	48

A la Fin ... Quelque Chose En Plus
At the End ... A Little Something Extra

Six Sauce Salées
Six Savory Sauces

Sauce au Pesto	Pesto Sauce	54
Sauce Vinaigrette	French Vinaigrette	55
Mayonnaise	French Mayonnaise	56
Sauce Béchamel	Classic White Sauce	57
Beurre Blanc	Wine & Butter Sauce	58
Aïoli	Garlic French Aioli	59

Six Sauce Sucrées
Six Sweet Sauces

Coulis Framboise	Fresh Raspberry Sauce	62
Sauce Caramel	Creamy Caramel Sauce	63
Coulis Chocolat	Rich Chocolate Sauce	64
Crème Anglaise	French-Style English Cream Sauce	65
Crème Patissière	Cream Puff Pastry Filling	66
Crème Chantilly	Whipped Cream	67

Amuses-Bouche
Appetite Prelude

Gougères
Cheese Puffs

*Lovely puffy melt-in-the-mouth appetizers that add elegance to your apéritif.
Especially delightful with a glass of French champagne.*

Serves: 6
Prep.:15 minutes Bake: 30 minutes

- 1 cup (20 cl) water
- 1/3 cup (90 grams) butter (reserve about 1 Tbsp. to grease muffin or mini muffin pan)
- 1tsp. salt, freshly ground pepper
- 3/4 cup (90 grams) flour
- 3 eggs, well beaten (reserve about 2 Tbsp. for brushing the tops)
- 4 tsp. (40 grams) grated good quality cheese (Cheddar, Comte)

Preheat oven to 400°F (200°C)

In a large saucepan add water, salt and butter.
Heat until butter is melted and completely mixed with the water.

Remove pan from stove and add the flour, beating rapidly and thoroughly, completely mixing into the water and butter.

Return the pan to the stove, rapidly stirring on low heat - about two minutes.

Remove pan from stove. Using mixer, add the beaten eggs to the flour/water/butter mixture.

Add grated cheese.

Beat mixture with mixer on high speed, about 2 minutes.

Drop teaspoons of batter into buttered cavities of a flexible (silicone)muffin pan.

Brush reserve beaten eggs over tops of each cheese puff.

Bake 25- 30 minutes until puffy and lightly browned.
Serve while warm.

Tip:
- **You** can prepare the dough a few hours in advance and keep it in the refrigerator before baking.
- **It** is also possible to freeze the dough in the flexible muffin pan.
- **After** they are frozen, pieces can be transferred to a freezer bag and kept in the freezer for a few months.
As desired,bake frozen pieces on a baking sheet for 35-40 minutes in the oven at 375 degrees.

Sablés au Parmiggiano
Cocktail Cheese Crackers

Flaky and crisp, these savory appetizer tidbits are especially delicious served warm out of the oven.

Serves: 6
Prep.: 15 minutes Bake: 10 minutes

- 1 cup (100 grams) flour
- 1 stick (100 grams) butter (room temperature)
- 1 cup (100 grams) shredded, good quality cheese(Parmesan or Aged Cheddar)
- 1 egg yolk

By hand, mix together flour, butter, shredded cheese and egg yolk.

Roll into a cylinder shape, about a 1" diameter log.

Wrap the roll in plastic food wrap and refrigerate 2 hours, minimum

Slice chilled log into thin, quarter-inch slices (5mm).

Place slices 1-inch (2,5cm) apart on ungreased cookie sheet. Bake in preheated 375 degrees oven (180C), 10 minutes until golden.

Tip:

Cool on oven pan. Lift and transfer each gently to avoid breaking/crumbling

Unbaked dough cylinder can be store tightly wrapped or in airtight container in the refrigerator 2-3 days before baking.

Pissaladière
French Pissaladiere

A specialty of Nice and Southern France, these oh-so-elegant and delicious small pizza-style tarts can be served as canapes when cut into pieces. Serve pissaladiere with a dry rosé from Provence and you can almost hear the sound of the cicadas...

Serves: about 6
Prep.: 30 minutes Bake: 20 minutes

- 5 Tbsp. olive oil
- 3 pounds (1 1/2 kilo) sliced onions
- 5 Tbsp. Herbs de Provence
- 12 oz.(300 grams) pizza crust, fresh or frozen
- 20 canned anchovy fillets, drained
- 20 pitted black olives in oil, drained
- Salt and pepper

Preheat oven to 400F (200°C)

Heat olive oil in a skillet over medium-low heat. Add sliced onions and stir frequently, until the onions become tender and start to turn golden (about 20 minutes).

Remove skillet from heat. Add Herbs de Provence.

Press the pizza crust into a rectangle on a 11 x 15 In. (30cm/40cm) baking sheet.

Reserving about 1/4 cup, spread cooked onions over crust, leaving 1 inch around the edges uncovered.

Bake tarte in the center of the oven, 15-20 minutes, until the crust is puffed, crispy and golden.

Remove from oven and decorate with reserved onion. Arrange anchovies in a crisscross pattern, adding an olive to the center of each shape.

Cut when slightly cooled. Serve warm or cold.

Rillettes de Sardines
Smoked Sardine Canapes

*This sardine spread is easy to prepare.
Enjoy as a tasty and healthy dip.*

Serves 6 as an appetizer.
Prep. : about 20 minutes

- 6 oz. (usually 2 cans total 200 grams) smoked sardines in olive oil, drained and filleted
- 2 Tbsp extra virgin olive oil
- 5 oz (150grams) cream cheese
- 1 lemon or lime, juiced
- 2-3 Tbsp. minced fresh herbs
- 10 pitted olives sliced in small pieces
- Salt and freshly ground pepper

Remove the sardines from the cans. Using a small, sharp knife, carefully slit open each fish, folding open to expose the backbone. Remove and discard the bones. Cut off and discard any tails. Set sardines aside.

In medium bowl, using a rubber spatula, mix cream cheese with olive oil. Add lemon juice, sliced olives and the fresh herbs, mix well until blended.

Add boneless sardines, mashing them into the cream mixture. Add salt and pepper to taste.

Tip:
- Can be served with toasted (gluten-free) bread or vegetables sticks.

- Chill prior to serving.

Gaspacho de Betterave
Beetroot Gazpacho

The ingredients in gazpacho are native to the Mediterranean region and sunny climates everywhere, from Seville, Spain to the South of France. Easy to prepare, serve gazpacho in small decorative glasses, dolloped with whipped cream. The red beets provide nutritional health benefits.

Serves: 6
Prep.: 20 minutes

- 1/2 pound (500 grams) chopped cooked beets
- 1 garlic clove, chopped
- 1 large sliced shallot
- 4 Tbsp. extra virgin olive oil
- 1 Tbsp. red wine vinegar
- 1 lemon, juiced
- 1 cup (250ml) mineral water
- Sea salt and pepper

Optional: heavy whipped cream, unsweetened

Place all ingrediens in a food processor and blend until smooth and well-mixed.

Add sea salt and pepper to taste.

Chill minimum 2 hours.

-Serve in small decorative glasses, dolloped with unsweetened whipped cream (page 67).

-You may top with crumbled cheese crackers (page 13).

Entrées

Appetizers

Salade Niçoise
Salad Nicoise

This classic salad is popular in Paris as well as the south of France. Serve in small portions as a first course. The protein-rich salad can be a meal in itself.

Serves: 6
Prep.: 30 minutes

- 6 or 7 oz. (200 grams) drained, canned tuna in oil
- 1 small lettuce or 7 oz. (200 grams) mesclun lettuce
- 12 cherry tomatoes
- 6 new potatoes, cooked and quartered lengthwise
- 3 eggs, cooked for 10 minutes in boiling water, cooled and halved
- 2 Tbsp finely chopped basil or 2 Tbsp. Basil Pesto (page 54)
- French Vinaigrette dressing (page 55)

Optional:
- 8 anchovy fillets cut lengthwise into thin strips
- 12 pitted olives, sliced

Prepare French Vinaigrette.

Place the tuna in a shallow dish and pour 1/3 of the dressing over it.

Lay the lettuce leaves onto 1 large plate or individual plates. Add: tomatoes, potatoes quartered, tuna and chopped basil. Drizzle the remaining dressing over the salad and add the egg slices.

Garnish with anchovy filets and sliced olives.
Serve immediately.

Tip:
Accompany with warm French baguette or toasted gluten-free bread.

Quiche Lorraine
Quiche Lorraine

Dating back to the 16th century, Quiche Lorraine is attributed to the unknown chef of Stanislaus, Duke of Lorraine. Warm and creamy, popular in France and around the world, Quiche Lorraine is a classic French dish. As an appetizer, cut into bite-size pieces and insert toothpicks or serve in wedges for a light meal.

Serves: 6 -8
Prep.:30 minutes Bake: 30 minutes

- 1 (8 oz. or 250 grams) frozen ready pastry pie shell.
- 3 slices (250 grams) bacon, diced
- 2 whole eggs + 2 egg yolks
- 1 cup (1/4 liter) whole milk
- 1 cup (1/4 liter) heavy whipping cream
- Salt, pepper
- dash grated nutmeg
- 1 1/2 cup (150 grams) grated gruyere, cheddar cheese or Swiss cheese, cubed

Preheat oven to 375F (190C).

Remove frozen pie shell from freezer while preparing the quiche ingredients. Pierce the dough with a fork a few times to keep it from rising.

Cut bacon into thin strips and sauté in skillet until crispy.

In a bowl, combine milk, cream, eggs and yolk. Season with salt and pepper. Add a dash of nutmeg.

Stir cooked bacon into egg mixture and pour into chilled pastry shell. Top with grated cheese.

Bake about 30 minutes until lightly browned.
Serve warm.

Tip:
Serve with a green salad.

Omelette aux fines herbes
Herbed Omelet

There's nothing like a perfectly cooked omelet that satisfies for any meal—breakfast, lunch or dinner. French comfort food at its best!

Serves: 4-6
Prep.: 15 minutes Cook.: 5 minutes

- 12 eggs, lightly beaten
- 2 Tbsp. (30 grams) unsalted butter + 1 Tbsp. canola oil
- 1/2 cup fines herbs (chopped chives and parsley)

Break the eggs into a medium mixing bowl. Season with salt and pepper.
Beat eggs lightly with a fork; add the chopped herbs.

Place oil and butter in a nonstick frying pan. When the butter is lightly browned, add the beaten eggs. Stir with a spatula. The omelet must be golden on the bottom and top barely cooked. Fold over and serve.

Tip:
You can replace fine herbs with:

Bacon/Ham:
- Add ½ cup (120 **grams**) meat: cooked bacon or finely chopped ham.

Mushrooms:
- Add 1 cup (200 **grams**) finely chopped cooked mushrooms (sautéed in 1Tsp. butter and 1Tbsp. olive oil).

Cheese:
- Add ½ cup (50 **grams**) shredded gruyere, mozzarella or cheddar cheese.

Soupe à l'Oignon
French Onion Soup

French Onion Soup is a classic! Savory soft onions in a tangy broth, topped with grated cheese, this soup is perfect for a winter menu appetizer or as a main dish.

Serves 6
Prep.: 20 minutes Cook.: 50 minutes

- 1/2 cup (120 grams) butter
- 6 medium yellow onions, (800g) thinly sliced onions
- 1 Tbsp. flour or gluten-free flour
- 8 cups (2 liters) hot water + 4 beef bouillon cubes
- 10-12 slices French baguette or gluten-free bread
- 8 oz. (250 grams) gruyere or emmental cheese finely grated

Melt butter in a stock pot on medium heat. Add onions and stir frequently until tender and golden brown (about 20 minutes). Add the flour, stirring until mixed in. Add water with beef bouillon cubes. bring to a boil. Reduce heat; cover and simmer for 30 minutes. Season with salt and pepper.

Turn on oven broiler. Cut two 1/2-inch (1cm) baguette slices for each serving. Place baguette/bread slices on a rimmed baking sheet in the center of the oven and toast until crisp and dry but not browned, about 1 minute per side.

Ladle soup into oven-safe serving bowls and place one or two slices of bread on top of each (bread may be broken into pieces if you prefer). Layer each slice of bread with grated cheese.

Place bowls on cookie sheet and broil in the preheated oven until cheese is melted and bubbling, about 5 minutes. Serve very hot.

Tip:
- Soup can be prepared and refrigerated for up to 3 days before serving (without cheese and toasts).

- Toast rounds can be prepared up to 3 days prior to serving. Store sealed at room temperature.

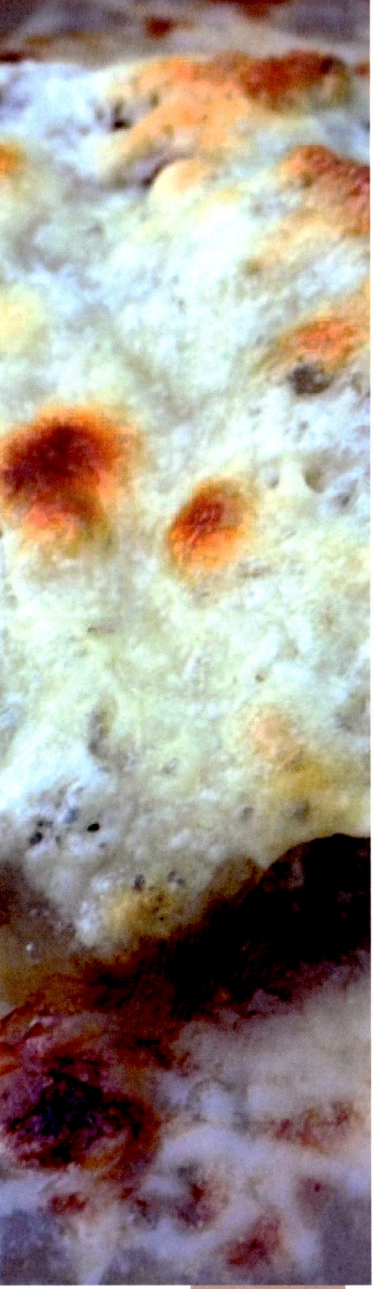

Velouté aux Champignons
Creamy Mushroom Soup

This rich and creamy soup is appealing in the fall and winter when a warm appetizer is especially appreciated.

Serves: 6
Prep.: 20 minutes Cook.: 20 minutes

- 1 pound (500 grams) sliced, fresh mushrooms
- 2 shallots, finely chopped
- 1/2 stick (60 grams) butter
- 4 cups (1 liter) whole milk
- Salt and pepper
- Pinch ground allspice
- 2 Tbsp. chopped parsley
- 3 Tbsp. roasted nuts

Brush the mushrooms clean, then finely slice.

Using medium heat, melt the butter in a pan and cook shallots until tender. Add mushrooms. Continue cooking on low heat, stirring occasionally about 10 more minutes, until soft.

Heat milk in microwave for 2 minutes.

Add hot milk to the cooked mushrooms. Cook 10 minutes over low heat, stirring occasionally.

Season to taste with sea salt, ground black pepper and allspice.

Blend with a hand mixer until smooth.

Pour into individual bowls. Garnish with parsley, chopped roasted nuts.

Serve immediately while very warm.

Tip:
Add 1 Tbsp. (15 grams) butter to the warm soup prior to serving.

Plats Principaux
Main Courses

Sole Meunière
Classic Sole Meuniere

Wikipedia defines the word meunière as «miller's wife». To cook something «à la meunière» is to first dredge it in flour, referring to its simple, rustic nature.

Serves: 4
Prep.: 15 min. Cook.: 6-8 min.

- 4 pieces sole fillets, boned and skinned
- 2/3 cup (80 grams) all-purpose flour or gluten-free flour
- 2 Tbsp.(30 grams) butter +1 Tbsp. olive oil
- 1/3 cup (80 grams) butter
- 1/2 lemon or lime, juiced
- 2 Tbsp. minced parsley
- Salt, pepper

Preheat oven to 225F (100°C).

Rinse sole and pat dry. Sprinkle each filet lightly with salt. Coat on all sides with flour, shaking off excess. Lay side by side on a plate.

In a frying pan, melt butter + oil over medium heat. When hot, lay the 4 fillets side by side. Cook fish on medium heat until browned on the bottom (1 1/2 to 2 minutes).

Using a wide, flexible spatula, gently turn fillets over to continue browning on the other side for an additional 1 to 2 minutes. If butter begins to scorch, reduce heat.

Using spatula, transfer fillets to an ovenproof platter, laying pieces side by side. Place into the preheated oven to keep fillets warm.

With a paper towel, wipe frying pan clean and return to medium heat. Add 1/3 cup butter, stir until melted.

Squeeze juice from 1/2 lemon into small bowl. Set aside.

Remove from heat, add lemon juice, and minced parsley. Mix well.

Using spatula, transfer fillets onto individual plates.

Immediately pour and scrape butter mixture over warm fish fillets.

Add additional salt to taste and serve.

Tip:
Serve with rice pilaf (p31), steamed baby potatoes or buttered pasta.

Saumon avec Riz Pilaf
Crispy Salmon with Rice Pilaf

You'll love the simplicity of this healthy and delicious main dish.

Serves: 4
Prep.: 10 min. Cook.: 5-6 min.

- 4 salmon filets with skin on one side
- 2 Tbsp. olive oil
- Salt, pepper, 1 Tbsp. minced parsley

Pour olive oil into a frying pan over medium heat. Once the oil is hot, add the salmon fillets, skin side down.

Cook for 5-6 minutes. The skin should be crispy and the inside cooked through. If preferred, leave the top slightly raw.

Add salt and pepper to taste. Garnish with parsley, if desired.

Serve warm with mashed potatoes or rice pilaf.

Rice Pilaf
Serves: 4
Prep 15 min. Cook/Bake 15-20 min

- 3 Tbsp.(45 grams) butter
- 1 medium onion, finely chopped
- 1 cups (200 grams) rice (basmati or Thai)
- 1 1/2 cups(350 ml) water + 1 fish bouillon cube
- 1 Tbsp.(15 grams) butter. Salt and Pepper

Preheat oven to 375 degrees F (180°C).

Melt the butter in a saucepan or skillet. Add the chopped onion and cook over medium heat, about 2 minutes.

Add rice to skillet and combine with onions.

Add water with fish cubes, bring to a boil and stir.

Season with salt and pepper.

Transfer to casserole dish.

Bake rice in the oven, 15 to 20 minutes. Remove from oven. Add salt and pepper, as necessary. Mix butter into rice and serve.

Tip:
Rice pilaf can accompany any fish or meat dish.

Boeuf Bourguignon
Beef Burgundy

Classic for a reason, Beef Burgundy remains one of the most popular French dishes. This hearty stew simmered in red wine creates a mouthwatering, irresistible aroma

Serves: 6 to 8
Prep.: 30 min. Cook.: 2 hours

- 3 pounds (1kg5) stewing meat, fat trimmed and cut into bite-size pieces
- 4 Tbsp. olive oil
- 1 onion, chopped
- 3-4 carrots, peeled and sliced diagonally
- 1/4 cup (30 grams) flour or gluten-free flour
- 3 cups (75 cl) red wine (reserve 1/3 cup wine to add before serving)
- 2 cups (50cl) boiling water + 2 beef bouillon cubes
- 2 garlic cloves, finely chopped
- Bouquet garni
- 4 slices cooked crispy bacon, cut in small pieces
- 2 Tbsp. (30 grams) butter
- 1/2 pound (250 grams) mushrooms, sliced
- Salt and pepper to taste

Heat oil in large skillet on medium heat. Add beef in batches and brown thoroughly.

In a soup pot, add browned beef, onions and carrots. Cook over medium heat, 2 -3 minutes. Blend in flour, stir and simmer about 3 minutes

Add wine, boiling water and bouillon cubes, chopped garlic, bouquet garni and salt. Give everything a good stir.

Bring to a boil then lower heat. Cover and simmer for about 2 hours, until meat is tender. Check regularly to ensure there is adequate liquid and the meat doesn't stick to the pan.

Melt butter in a skillet over medium heat. Add sliced mushrooms and cook for a few minutes until mushrooms are cooked through. Adjust seasonings, to taste.

Add mushrooms, crispy bacon and 1/3 cup wine to soup pot. Simmer uncovered over low heat for 10 minutes.
If necessary, salt and pepper to taste.

Tip:
Serve with steamed baby potatoes or tagliatelles (wide egg butter noodles).

Pot au Feu
Beef Brisket with Vegetables

Pot au Feu is a traditional hearty and healthy French winter dish. Easy to prepare, simply toss the beef and chopped vegetables into a large pot and simmer for several hours.

Serves: 6 to 8
Prep.: 20 min. Cook.: 4-5 hours

- 1 gallon(4 liters) water + 2 Tbsp. salt
- 4 pounds (2 kilos) beef brisket + (optional) 3 or 4 pieces bone-in beef short ribs
- 3 celery stalks, washed and chopped
- 2 onions, quartered
- 1 bouquet garni
- 1 head of garlic, peeled and halved crosswise
- 6 carrots, washed, peeled and sliced in half, lengthwise. Cut each slice in half
- 2 pounds (1 kilo) potatoes
- Salt and pepper

Bring water to a boil in a very large heavy pot. Place brisket and short ribs in the pot.

Add chopped celery, quartered onions, bouquet garni, garlic and salt.

Cover, reduce heat and simmer on low heat for 3 to 4 hours (until meat is tender). Remove meat and bones and set aside. Using a sieve, remove celery, onions, bouquet garni and garlic from the broth.

Return broth to a boil; add potatoes and carrots.
Simmer until vegetables are tender but not mushy, about 10 minutes.

Transfer vegetables and meat to a serving platter. Spoon some broth over meat and vegetables.

Tip:
- Serve with horseradish, mustard or mayonnaise (page 56) in small bowls as an accompaniment.

- Serve with warmed or toasted baguette.

- Leftover broth can be frozen for future use.

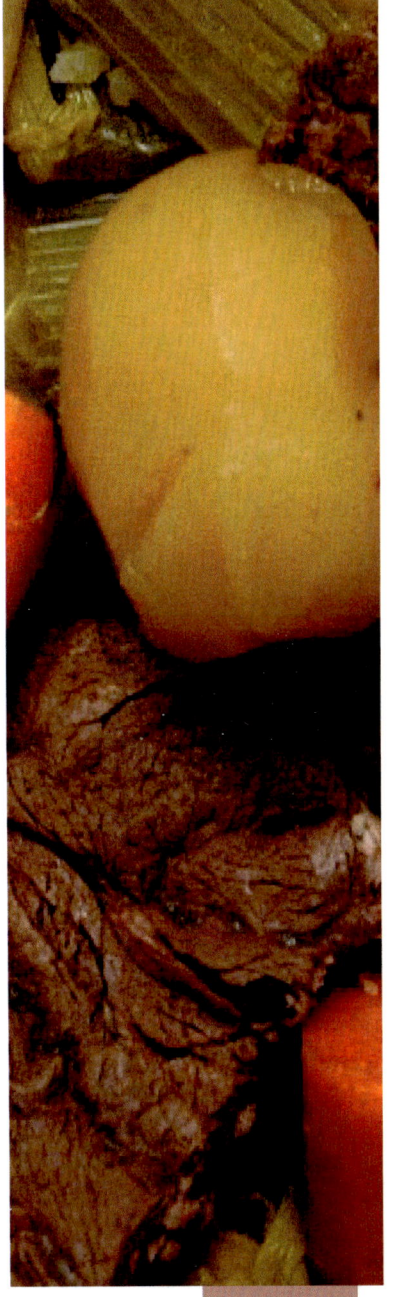

Parmentier de Canard
Duck and Potato Casserole

The French word "parmentier" means cooked with potatoes. This hearty dish is easy to prepare, delicious and filling.

Serves: 4 to 6
Prep: 15 min. Bake: 1 hour

- 4 duck confit legs (Available in gourmet shops or Amazon.com)
- 2 shallots, finely chopped
- 1 box 48 oz (1,3 kg) Idaho Buttery Homestyle or Mashed Potatoes (gluten-free option, next page)
- 1 Tbsp. (15 grams) butter
- 1 cup (100 grams) grated cheddar, gruyere or parmesan cheese
- Salt and pepper

Preheat oven to 250°F (120°C).

Heat the duck legs gently -low heat- in a pan for 1 hour.

Remove cooked duck legs skin and wipe dry.

Save the confit fat to use for browning the shallots.

In a bowl, shred the duck meat with a fork. Place shredded meat on a plate. Using the same pan or skillet, brown shallots in 2 tsp reserved confit fat. Add shredded meat. Cook on medium heat until the meat is golden brown, 4-5 minutes.

Prepare boxed mashed potatoes according to directions or prepare fresh mashed potatoes (see recipe, page 33).
Butter a baking dish or casserole.

Layer half the duck meat on bottom and then a layer of potatoes.

Mash the remainder of the duck meat and spread over mixture. Top with remaining mashed potatoes. Bake 40 minutes.

Before serving, sprinkle with grated cheese and bake 5 minutes, until golden. Serve warm.

Tip:
Serve hot with a mixed green salad.

Purée de Pomme de Terre
French Potato Puree

Popular with the French as well as Americans, this homemade side dish is scrumptious.

Serves: 6
Prep: 15 min. Cook.: 20-25 min

- 2 pounds (1 kilo) washed, unpeeled potatoes (about the same size)
- 3/4 cup (200 grams) cold butter
- 1 cup (250 ml) boiling whole milk
- Salt and pepper

Place whole potatoes in cold water. Add 2 tsp salt.

Bring to a boil and cook 20-25 minutes, until tender.

Remove potatoes from hot water. Allow to cool slightly, and then peel.

Using a hand masher, mash the potatoes in a mixing bowl. Add the cold butter (cut into small pieces) and boiling milk; mix well.

Season with salt and pepper to taste.

Tip:
- Goes well with any fish or meat.

- Can be prepared several hours in advance. Refrigerate and warm in microwave before serving.

Desserts
Desserts

Crème Brûlée
Classic Crème Brûlée

Exceptionally rich, vanilla-infused classic French dessert

Serves: 4 to 6
Prep. :20 min. Bake: 35 min.

- 2 cups (50 cl) boiling heavy cream or Half and Half
- 2 tsp vanilla extract
- 6 egg yolks
- 1/2 cup (100 grams) granulated sugar
- 6 Tbsp. brown sugar for topping

Preheat the oven to 325°F (160°C).

Pour cream into small saucepan. Add vanilla extract. Bring to a gentle simmer over medium heat until it almost comes to boil. Remove from heat.

In mixing bowl, beat egg yolks and sugar until well-blended.

Slowly pour the boiling cream into the yolk mixture, stirring well to combine. Pour, dividing mixture equally in 6 ovenproof ramekins.

Place ramekins in a deep roasting pan. Fill pan with boiling water until filled halfway up the sides of the ramekins. Bake 30 to 35 minutes or until the center is barely set. Remove from the oven. Cool at room temperature, then refrigerate until cool, at least 2 hours or overnight.

When ready to serve, sprinkle each dish with 1 Tbsp brown sugar and use a blowtorch to caramelize the top.

Alternatively, place the sugar-topped custard dishes under the oven broiler, keeping a close eye on them to ensure the sugar doesn't burn.

The topping should be a lovely golden color.
Allow the sugar to cool (about 1 minute)until hardened and serve.

Tip:
- For chocolate crème brulee, replace vanilla extract with 2 Tbsp. chocolate powder.

- For lime crème brulee, replace vanilla extract with 1 fresh lime zest.

Fondant Chocolat
Molten Chocolate Cakes

This warm, soft-centered chocolate dessert is a delight.

Serves: 6
Prep.: 30 min. Bake: 10-12 min.

- 2 Tbsp. (30 grams) melted butter for brushing
- 5 oz. (150 grams) good quality dark chocolate, broken into pieces
- 1 stick (110 grams) butter
- 1/2 cup (100 grams) granulated sugar
- 4 large eggs
- 1/4 cup (30 grams) flour or gluten-free flour or corn starch

Preheat oven to 400°F (200°C).

To get your Molten Chocolate Cakes to come out perfectly from the non-stick silicon pan, trace the outline of the cake pan onto parchment paper and cut it out. Grease each cavity. Line the greased bottom of the molds with the parchment paper, press well. Thoroughly grease/butter each cavity again

Place chocolate and butter in a bowl set over a saucepan of simmering water (or use a double boiler). Warm and stir until smooth (about 4 minutes). Allow to cool slightly.

Combine sugar and eggs in mixing bowl and whisk until pale and fluffy. Gently fold in the melted chocolate mixture and then the flour.
Fold lightly until well combined.
Evenly portion the warm mixture into the 6 buttered molds. Place molds on baking sheet; bake 10-13 minutes. The outside will be cooked and the center will be molten. Remove from oven and let stand about 10 minutes.
Run a palette knife around edge of the chocolate cakes to release. Carefully turn over molds, transferring to individual serving dishes or shallow bowls. Remove the parchment paper.

Tip:
- For ginger-flavor Molten Cakes: Add 2 oz. (60 grams) candied ginger, minced.
- Add a scoop of vanilla ice cream or whipped cream and garnish with berries, if desired.
- Molten Chocolate Cakes can be prepared in advance and baked prior to serving.

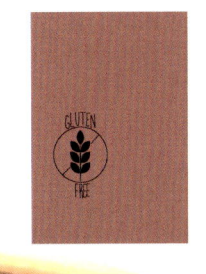

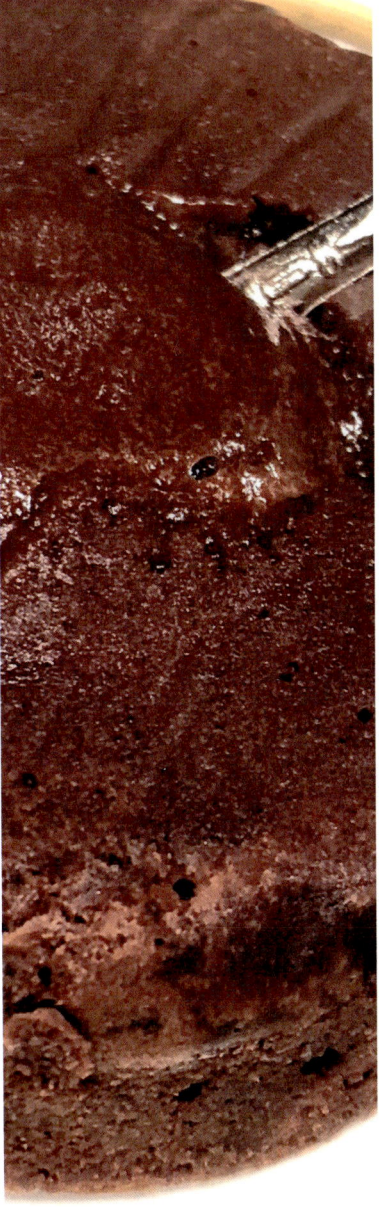

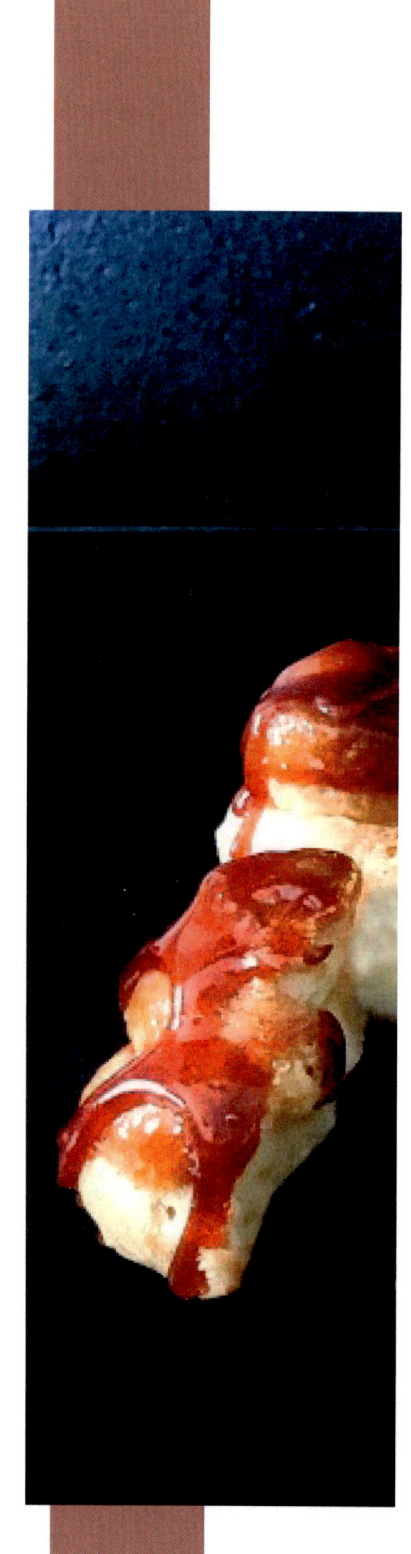

Chou à la Crème
Cream Puff Pastry

Cream puffs and éclairs are easy to make. These pastries can be filled with Crème Chantilly (p.67) or Crème Pâtissière (p.66).

Serves: 6 to 8
Prep.: 30 min. Bake: 30 min.

- 1 cup (1/4 liter) water
- 1/3 cup (90 grams) butter
- 3/4 cup (90 grams) flour
- 3 eggs, well beaten (reserve about 1 Tbsp. for brushing the tops)
- 1 tsp. salt
- 1 tsp. granulated sugar

Preheat oven to 375F (190°C).

In a large saucepan, add butter, water, salt and sugar. Heat until butter is melted, stirring until completely mixed.

Remove pan from heat and add the flour, beating rapidly and thoroughly, completely mixing into the water and butter.

Return the pan to the stove and continue stirring rapidly on low heat, about 2 minutes.

Remove pan from stove. Beat eggs, one at a time, into the flour/water/butter mixture.
Beat mixture about 1 more minute.

Drop by rounded teaspoonfuls 2 inches apart onto greased baking sheets.

Bake until puffs rise and are golden brown, about 30 minutes.

Before removing, turn oven off, prop oven door open with wooden spoon to permit moisture to escape, about 1 minutes. Cool baking sheets on wire racks.

Cut each puff horizontally and fill with crème pâtissière (p66).

Tip:
- Before serving, drizzle with warm caramel sauce (p. 63)
- For rich profiteroles, fill with vanilla ice cream and top with chocolate sauce (recipe, p. 64)
- Can be stored in refrigerator up to 2 days prior to serving

Île Flottante
Floating Island

Creamy and crunchy, Floating Island makes a grand finale to any dinner. It was a family tradition that her mother made this dessert on Sundays and it remains a favorite with Yolande, her sisters and her husband, Jean-Claude.

Serves: 6
Prep.: 10 min. Bake:10 min.

- Prepared Crème Anglaise (page 65)
- Prepared Caramel sauce (page 63)

Meringues:
- 1/2 cup(100 grams) granulated sugar
- 4 large egg whites, room temperature

Preheat oven to 350F (180°C).

Using electric mixer, beat egg whites on medium speed until frothy. On high speed, gradually add powdered sugar. Beat until very stiff and glossy.
To get your meringues to come out perfectly from the muffin non-stick silicon pan cavities, trace the outline of the bottom of the muffin pan cavity onto parchment paper. Cut one per cavity. Grease each cavity then press parchment paper circles into each cavity. Butter/grease each again. Gently spoon egg meringue mixture into each cavity, dividing equally.

Bake 8-10 minutes. Remove muffin pan from oven and, while warm, run a palette knife around edge of the meringue to release.

Carefully remove each onto a sheet of parchment paper. Set aside at room temperature (up to 4 hours) until serving.

Before plating meringues, pour Crème Anglaise over bottom of bowls or dessert plates.

Place a meringue on top of each serving and drizzle with Caramel Sauce.

Tip:
Floating island can be prepared 1 day in advance.

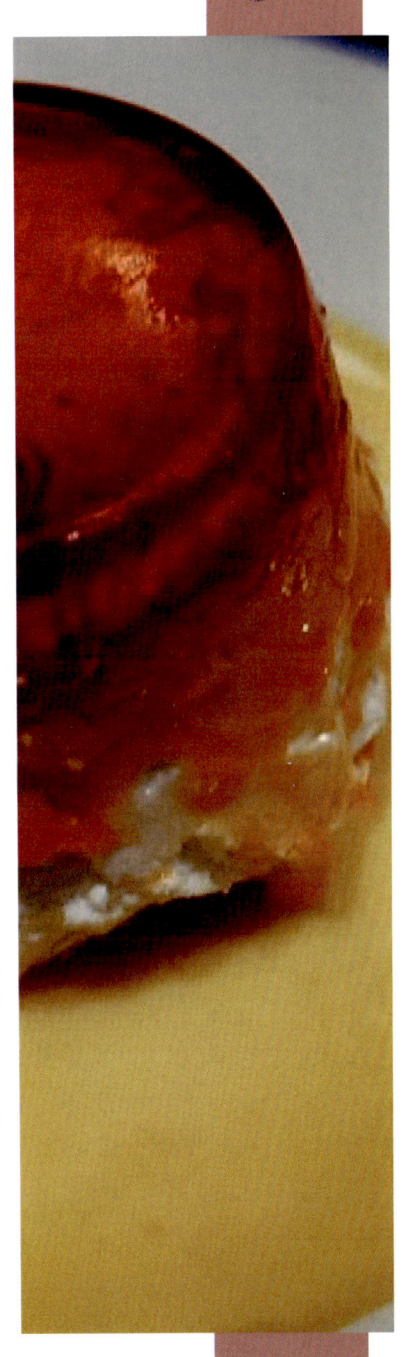

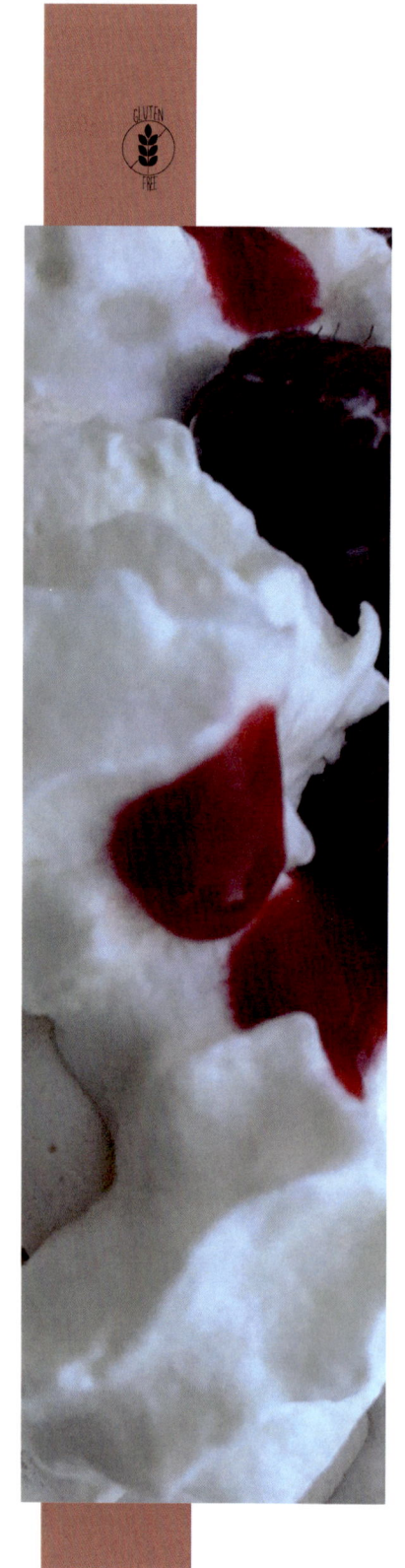

Pavlova

Named for the famous Russian ballerina Anna Pavlova, this light and airy dessert is perfect for warm summer evenings.

Serves: 6
Prep.: 20 min Bake: 1 1/2 hours.

- 4 egg whites (150 grams), room temperature
- 1 1/2 cups (300 grams) granulated sugar
- 1 tsp. white wine vinegar
- 1 Tbsp. corn starch
- 1 tsp. vanilla extract
- 1 1/2 cups (150 grams) : your choice berries (Halved strawberries, blueberries, raspberries)
- 1 1/2 cups (300 grams) whipping cream (page 67)
- Vanilla ice cream

Preheat oven to 275 F (130°C). Line baking sheets with parchment or wax paper.

To prepare meringue:
Separate egg yolks and whites. Discard yolks. Pour egg whites into large mixing bowl. Using electric hand mixer beat on medium speed until eggs resemble a fluffy cloud and stand up in stiff peaks when mixer blades are lifted. Increase speed, gradually adding sugar. Continue beating for 3-4 seconds between each addition.

When the mixture has thickened, add vinegar, corn starch and vanilla, continuing to beat briskly (about 1 minute) until completely mixed and firm.

Draw 6 circles of approximately 10 cm / 4-inch diameter (using a glass as a guide) on wax or parchment paper. Spoon and spread meringue in each circle to fit the dimensions.

Using the back of a spoon, make a shallow crater in the center so the edges will be curved upward to hold the berries.

Bake for about 1 1/2 hours until the meringues are crisp outside and creamy inside.

Plate each Pavlova and add a scoop of vanilla ice cream in the indented center. Dollop a generous amount of whipped cream (page 67), then top with berries. Serve immediately.

Tip:
Before removing, turn oven off, prop oven door open with wooden spoon to permit moisture to escape, about 15 minutes.

L'Heure du Thé
Teatime Treats

Madeleines au chocolat
Chocolate Madeleines

According to French legend, in 1755, Louis XV was charmed by the little cakes prepared by Madeleine Paulmier and named them after her. Served at Versailles they became a favorite throughout France.

Serves: about 15 pieces
Prep.: 30 min. Bake: 10-12 min.

- 2/3 cup (160 grams) butter
- 2 eggs
- 1/2 cup (100 grams) granulated sugar
- 3/4 cup (95 grams) flour or gluten-free flour
- 1/2 tsp. baking powder or gluten-free baking powder
- 1/4 cup (30 grams) cocoa powder
- 2 Tbsp. milk
- Silicone Madeleine baking pan

Preheat oven to 400 °F (200°C). Butter madeleine non-stick silicon pan, refrigerate 5 minutes.

In a small, heavy-bottomed saucepan, melt remaining butter over medium heat. Continue to cook until butter turns golden, being careful not to let the butter burn. Remove from heat and strain through a fine mesh sieve into a small bowl; set aside.

In a medium bowl (use electric mixer fitted with the whisk attachment) to whip 2 eggs and granulated sugar until light and thickened, about 2 minutes.

Add flour, baking powder, cocoa and milk. Stir on low speed until combined. *mix in butter.*

Using a teaspoon, fill Madeleine shells with batter. Bake until Madeleines are puffed in the middle, 10-12 minutes.

Cool pan on baking rack. Remove cookies and set aside. Wipe any remaining crumbs out of cavities in pan.

Chocolate-Coated Madeleines

- 3 oz. (100 grams) baking chocolate
- 2 tsp. peanut oil.

Melt baking chocolate with oil over double boiler with simmering water. When completely melted and well mixed use small pastry brush and coat a thin layer of melted chocolate covering each cavity.

Immediately place baked Madeleines carefully into each cavity, pressing lightly into the chocolate.

Refrigerate until the chocolate has cooled and hardened slightly (minimum 1 hour).

Financier
French Financier Cakes

Classic little pastries you see in the windows of Paris bakeries.

Serves: 6
Prep.: 30 min. Bake: 15 min.

- 2/3 cup (150 grams) butter
- 3/4 cup (150 grams) granulated sugar
- 1 cup (120 grams) almond flour
- 1/2 cup (50 grams) flour or cornstarch
- 5 egg whites
- 1 tsp. vanilla extract or 1 Tbsp. orange marmalade or 1 Tbsp chocolate powder

Preheat oven to 375 F (190°C).

Place the butter in a small pan and melt thoroughly on low heat until the butter starts to bubble and brown slightly. Remove from heat and strain through a fine mesh sieve into a small bowl; set aside.

Combine dry ingredients: granulated sugar, almond flour and cornstarch in mixing bowl. Add egg whites and flavoring (vanilla extract or orange marmalade or chocolate powder). Fold in the butter mixture. Combine well.

Spoon batter into financier silicone pan (or any buttered pan with small cavities).

Place the tray in the center of the oven.

Bake for 15 minutes; remove from oven (financiers will seem a little soft).

Cool in pan at least 10 minutes before removing.

Tip:
Serve with tea, coffee or Crème Anglaise.

Quatre Quart
Fluted Mini Pound Cakes

These cute and flavorful little cakes can be held daintily to dip into coffee or milk.

Serves: 6 to 8
Prep.:15 min. Bake: 30 min.

- 3/4 cup butter (200 grams) at room temperature
- 1 cup (200 grams) granulated sugar
- 2 tsp. vanilla extract
- 3 eggs
- 1 1/2 cups (200 grams) all-purpose flour or gluten-free flour

Preheat oven to 375 F (190°C).

Cream butter, sugar, eggs and vanilla.

Add flour. Mix well.

Pour batter into a buttered non-stick silicon flexible cup cake pan. Bake until a toothpick inserted in center comes out wih a few moist crumbs attached, about 30 minutes

Tip:

-For chocolate flavor: eliminate vanilla and substitute 2 Tbsp. (35g) cocoa powder.

-For orange flavor: eliminate vanilla, reduce sugar to ½ cup (100 g) and substitute 3 Tbsp. orange marmalade.

-For pistachio flavor, eliminate vanilla and substitute 2 Tbsp. pistachio paste.

Les Gâteaux de Maman
Mama's Little Cakes

Throughout Yolande's childhood, her mother often baked these simple little cakes. This recipe remains a favorite with Yolande and her sisters. Serve with mixed fruit or custard.

Serves: 6 to 8
Prep.: 20 min. Bake: 20 min.

- 2 sticks (250 grams) butter
- 1 cup (200 grams) granulated sugar
- 2 eggs
- 1 tsp. vanilla extract
- 1 cup (120 grams) flour or corn flour or gluten-free flour
- 1 cup (120 grams) almond powder
- 1 tsp. baking powder or gluten-free baking powder

Preheat oven to 375 F (180°C).

Cream butter, sugar, eggs and vanilla. Add flour or corn flour or gluten-free flour, almond powder and baking powder. Mix well together.

To get your cakes to release perfectly, first trace the outline of the non-stick silicon cupcake pan cavity on parchment paper. Cut out each paper shape and press firmly onto the greased bottom of each cavity. After the paper is placed on the bottom, butter each cavity thoroughly. Pour batter into each cavity, dividing equally.

Bake 20 minutes. Remove from oven and let stand about 10 minutes.
Run a palette knife around edge of the little cakes to release. Carefully turn over cakes, transferring to a serving plate. Remove the parchment paper.

Tip:
-For chocolate flavor: eliminate vanilla and substitute 2 Tbsp. (35g) cocoa powder.

- For citrus flavor, eliminate vanilla and substitute 1 Tbsp. lemon zest.

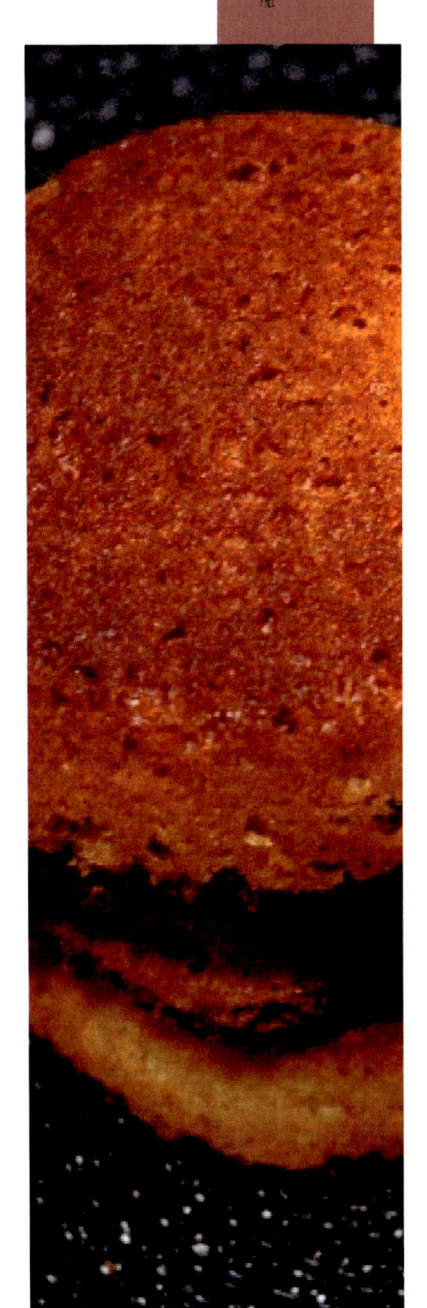

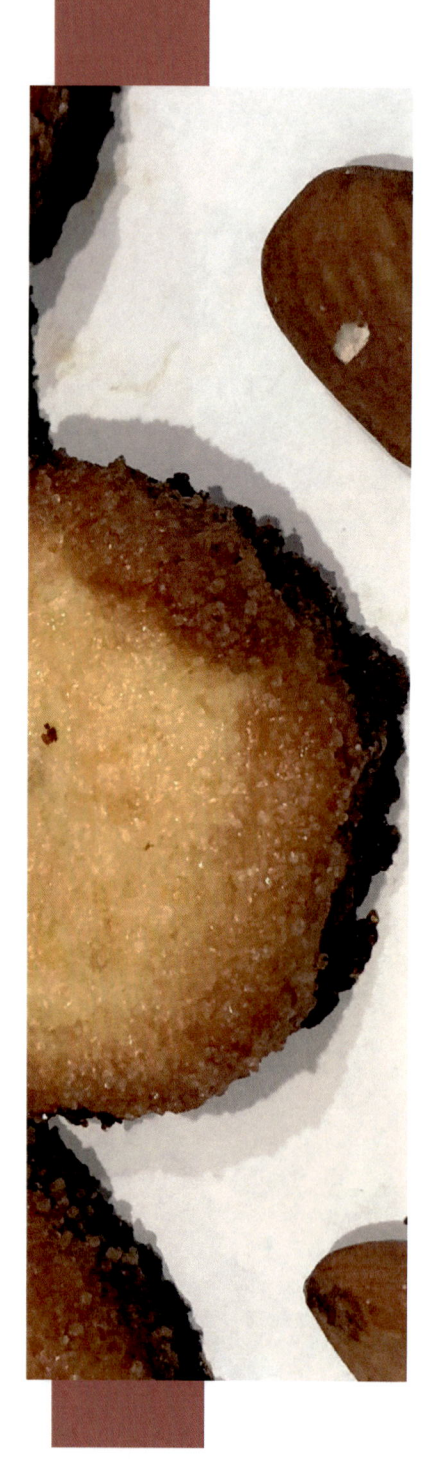

Sablés Diamants
Diamond Butter Cookies

Diamonds are everyone's best friend when they delight your taste buds and melt in your mouth in sweet, buttery bites.

Serves: 6 to 8 (24 pieces)
Prep.:15 min. Bake: 10-12 min.

- 1 1/2 sticks (150 grams) butter softened at room temperature
- 3/4 cup (75 grams) confectioners sugar
- 2 egg yolks
- 1 1/2 cups (200 grams) flour
- 1 tsp. vanilla extract
- 1 cup (160 grams) clear sugar crystals
- 1 beaten egg

Cream together butter and confectioner's sugar until smooth. Beat in egg yolks, one at a time: stir in vanilla and flour. Shape dough into a log, 1" diameter.

Refrigerate minimum 3 hours.

Beat whole egg; roll log in egg mixture. Roll log carefully in crystal sugar and repeat, 2 times. Make sure the sugar adheres to the dough.

Preheat oven to 400F (200°C).

Slice dough into 1/4 inch rounds. Place 1 inch apart on parchment paper on baking sheet.

Bake 10 to 12 minutes or until cookies are just beginning to brown around the edges.

Tip:

-Cookies are especially delicious when served warm.

-Can be prepared up to 4 days in advance. Roll in plastic wrap and refrigerate. Slice and bake just before serving.

-Store in airtight container 5-7 days.

A la Fin...
Quelque Chose En Plus

At the End...
A Little Something Extra

Six Sauces Salées

Six Savory Sauces

Sauce au Pesto
Pesto Sauce

Pesto is easy to prepare and much more flavorful than commercial versions. With the aroma of Provence, pesto is piquant with pasta, on salad or spread on toast as an appetizer.

Makes about 1 cup
Prep.: 15 min.

- 1/3 cup pine nuts, lightly toasted
- 1/2 cup extra-virgin olive oil
- 2 garlic cloves
- 2 cups (60 grams) fresh basil leaves
- 1/2 cup grated Parmesan cheese
- Salt, pepper

Pulse pine nuts in a food processor until pulverized.

Scrape the sides of the bowl with a spatula. Add olive oil and garlic and continue pulsing until garlic is finely chopped.

On a cutting board, chop basil coarsely, cutting leaves into halves or thirds with a knife. Add to food processor. Pulse until basil is entirely mixed into the oil, occasionally stopping to push leaves down using a rubber scraper.

Pour pesto mixture into a bowl and add parmesan cheese and salt. Stir to combine; adjust salt and pepper to taste.

Tip:

- Pesto can be frozen in small portions. Defrost and use as a garnish for grilled or roasted meat or fish or with vegetables.

- Pesto makes a wonderful sauce substitute for marinara over cooked pasta.

- For a thinner sauce, add 2-3 additional Tbsp. olive oil.

- Refrigerate in airtight container up to 3 days. Add additional oil to top of pesto prior to refrigerating.

Vinaigrette
French Vinaigrette

Homemade classic French vinaigrette dressing for your mixed green salad.

Serves: 4 to 6
Prep.: 5 to 10 min.

- 1 tsp. mustard
- 6 Tbsp virgin olive oil
- 2 Tbsp. vinegar (white, wine, or cider)
- 1 garlic clove, finely chopped
- 1 Tbsp. parsley, finely chopped
- Salt, pepper

Mix mustard, olive oil, vinegar, garlic, parsley, salt and pepper in a medium mixing bowl. Stir until well combined.

Just before serving, taste vinaigrette and add salt and pepper if needed. Mix thoroughly.

Dress salad and serve immediately.

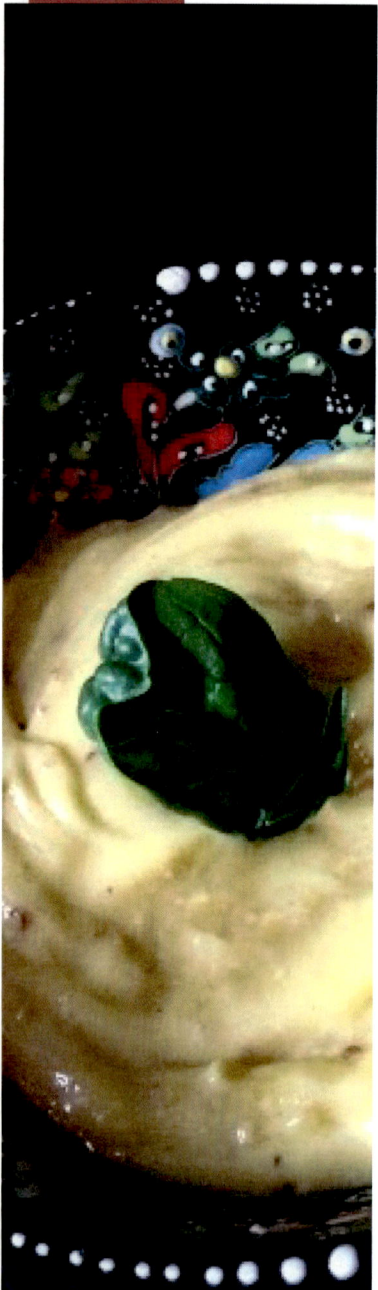

Mayonnaise
French Mayonnaise

Your own crafted mayonnaise beats the jar version, hands-down. Tuna and chicken salad will taste especially delectable using this authentic French recipe.

Serves: 4
Prep.: 15 min.

- 1 large egg yolk or 2 small egg yolks
- 1 tsp. French mustard (Dijon)
- 1 Tbsp. lemon juice or vinegar
- 3/4 cup (200 ml) sunflower oil or olive oil
- 1tsp. salt and 1tsp. white pepper

Let all the ingredients sit at room temperature for approximately 30 minutes prior to preparation. This helps the process of emulsification.

Using a wire whisk, gently mix egg yolk(s), Dijon mustard and lemon juice (or vinegar).

Drip the oil slowly into the mixing bowl while continuing to whisk briskly.
When mixture has begun to thicken, increase the rate of the pour.

Continue stirring vigorously while adding the remaining oil

Add salt and pepper to taste.

Transfer the mayonnaise into a glass, ceramic or plastic container. Be sure to keep the mayonnaise covered tightly and refrigerated following preparation.

Tip:
- If your mayonnaise "breaks", take a fresh egg yolk and slowly beat mayonnaise into the yolk. (The fresh yolk will re-emulsify the sauce and hold it together).

- Mayonnaise can be refrigerated up to 2 days

- Mayonnaise is the base of many sauces.
For cocktail sauce: 1/2 cup of mayonnaise, 1 Tbsp. ketchup, 1 tsp. cognac, 1tsp. Worcestershire sauce, 5 drops tabasco hot pepper sauce

Béchamel
Classic White Sauce

Béchamel sauce is easy to prepare and elevates cooked potatoes and vegetables.

Serves:4
Prep.: 15 min.

- 2 Tbsp. (25 grams)) butter
- 3 Tbsp. (25 grams)) flour or gluten-free flour
- 2 cups (1/2 liter) whole milk, warmed
- Salt and white pepper

Melt butter in saucepan on a low heat. Gradually add flour, stirring continuously for 1 minute.

Increase heat to medium. Gradually add warm milk, stirring continuously until boiling.

Lower heat and continue stirring to avoid lumps from forming or burning. Sauce will thicken, becoming creamy and unctuous.

Season with salt and white pepper.

Tip:
- Substitute Béchamel for marinara sauce in lasagna or on pasta dishes.

- Try it on potatoes, carrots and cauliflower. Sprinkle with grated gruyere cheese and bake 5 minutes, until golden.

Beurre Blanc
Wine & Butter Sauce

A staple in French cooking, Beurre Blanc is best prepared with white wine to accompany fish. Use red wine instead of white for meat dishes.

Serves: 6
Prep.: 15 min.

- 1 cup (240 grams) cold butter, cut into tablespoons
- 1 medium shallot, finely minced
- 1/4 cup (65 ml) dry white wine (for fish) or red wine (for meat)
- 1 Tbsp. vinegar
- Salt and freshly ground pepper

Optional:
- 1 Tbsp. fresh chopped fine herbs (basil, parsley, and chives)
- 1 tsp. lemon juice

In small saucepan, combine shallots, wine and vinegar over medium heat.

Bring to a boil, decrease heat and simmer until liquid reduced to 2 Tbsp., about 2 minutes.

Turn down heat to lowest setting. Whisk in butter, 1 Tbsp at a time, adding another piece as the previous piece melted. Don't allow sauce to become too hot.

Season with salt and pepper and keep warm.

Just before serving, stir in herbs and lemon juice.

Tip:
- If your sauce does «break» because it's gotten too hot. Take a bowl and put 1 Tbsp cold water in the bottom.
 While whisking constantly, slowly pour the broken sauce into the bowl with the water.
 Serve immediatly or return to low heat if needed.

- Perfect with sautéed mushrooms, cooked asparagus or steamed fish.

Aïoli
Garlic French Aioli

With its origins in Provence in the south of France, Aioli is a rich, garlicy mayonnaise that adds a tangy zip to legumes and fish

Serves: 6
Prep.: 20 min.

- 1 medium potato, baked and peeled
- 2 egg yolks
- 1 cup virgin olive oil
- Salt to taste (about 1/2 teaspoon)
- 4-6 garlic cloves, peeled and crushed in garlic press

In a bowl, mash the potato thoroughly with garlic and salt until it becomes a smooth paste.

Add the egg yolks and mix well. Drip the oil slowly into the mixing bowl while continuing to blend briskly.

After all oil has been mixed thoroughly and the aioli is thick, add salt to taste.

Refrigerate maximum 2 days before serving.

Tip:
Aioli is a tangy versatile sauce that enhances chicken as well as fish and vegetables.

Six Sauces Sucrées

Six Sweet Sauces

Coulis Framboise
Fresh Raspberry Sauce

Fresh raspberry puree adds a tart and pretty garnish to ice cream and cakes. Made without preservatives, the puree can be frozen in small portions to use as desired.

Serves: 6
Prep.: 20 to 30 min.

- 1 pound (500 grams) fresh or frozen raspberries
- 1/2 cup (100 grams) granulated sugar
- 1 Tbsp. lemon juice

Place washed raspberries in food processor. Blend until smooth, 3-5 minutes.

In mixing bowl, press blended berries through fine mesh sieve to remove seeds.
Add sugar and lemon juice; mix well.

Pour the mixture into saucepan, using rubber spatula. Serve.

Can be refrigerated up to 5 days. If desired, freeze in small portions and defrost 12 hours prior to serving or microwave on defrost setting.

Tip:
Drizzle in elegant swirls over vanilla ice cream or cakes.

Sauce Caramel
Creamy Caramel Sauce

Mmmmm... Who doesn't love creamy caramel topping on ice cream, fruit or cake?

Serves: 6
Prep.: 20 min.

- 1/2 cup (125ml) whipping cream
- 1/2 cup (100 grams) granulated sugar
- 1 Tbsp. water
- 1/4 cup (60 grams) butter
- Pinch salt

Warm whipping cream in microwave for 1 minute.

In heavy saucepan, heat sugar and water on moderate heat.

As the sugar begins to melt, stir gently with a wooden spoon.

When mixture starts to boil, stop stirring but leave on heat until the mixture turns amber in color. Immediately remove pan from heat.

Add butter to the mixture , stirring until butter is completely melted.

Slowly add warmed whipping cream to the pan, stir to blend. The mixture will foam considerably. Continue stirring until caramel is smooth.

Cool in saucepan, minimum 30 minutes.

Pour into glass container and cool until room temperature. Refrigerate up to 1 week.

Warm before serving.

Tip:
Serve over ice cream, cake, or fresh fruit.

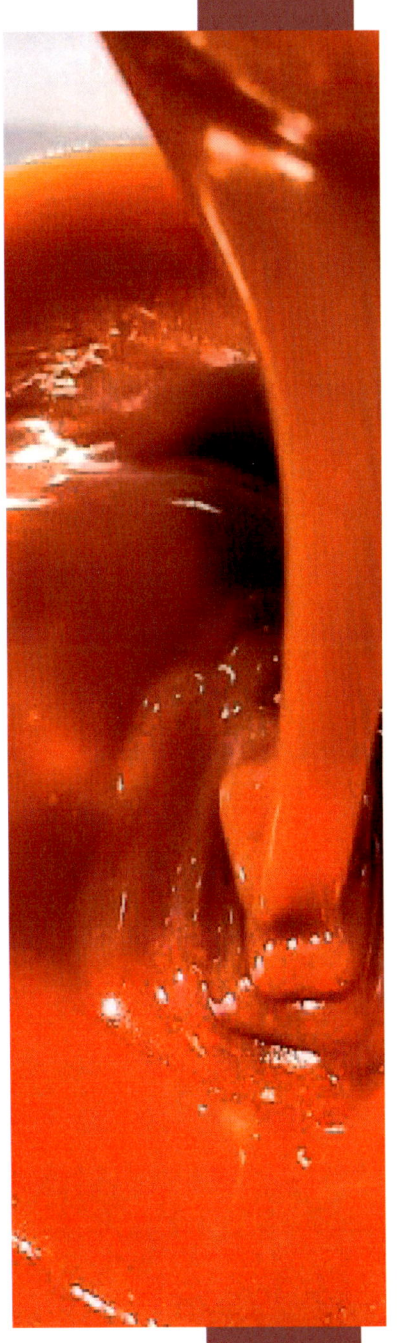

Coulis Chocolat
Chocolate Sauce

In any language, chocolate is a favorite! This rich chocolate is widely used for French pastries and as a topping for ice cream, cake or fresh fruit. This recipe is perfect for chocolate fountains.

Serves: 6
Prep.: 15 min.

- 3/4 cup (200 ml) Half and Half
- 2 cups (200 grams) dark chopped chocolate or cocoa powder

Optional: 1Tbsp. granulated sugar

In a medium saucepan, warm the whipping cream and chocolate over medium heat, whisking continuously until boiling. Add butter and sugar.

At boiling point, stir the chocolate and cream mixture until smooth; remove from heat.

Serve warm.

Tip:

- You may add 1 Tbsp mineral water to obtain a more creamy consistancy

- Refrigerate up to 5 days in glass jar with lid.

- Swirl over ice cream, cake or pastries.

- For profiteroles, make cream puff pastry (p. 38). Slice each in half. Fill with vanilla ice cream and top with chocolate sauce.

Crème Anglaise
French-Style English Cream Sauce

Like béchamel and pastry cream, this custard is a basic of French cuisine. The English (Anglaise) custard cream version has been popular since the 16th century (when it was thicker and served warm). The French version omits flour and this cream is usually served cold as an accompaniment to pastries like madeleines (p.44) and financiers (p.45). Yolande's mother served Crème Anglaise with meringues as the dessert called «Floating Island» (P.39)

Serves: 6
Prep.: 20 min. Cook.: 2-3 min.

- 1/2 cup (100 grams)) granulated sugar
- 4 egg yolks
- 2 cups (1/2 liter) milk
- 2 tsp. vanilla extract

In medium mixing bowl, stir sugar and egg yolks together until blended.

In medium saucepan, add milk and sugar and egg yolk mixture. Warm ingredients on medium heat, just below boiling. As mixture thickens, the consistency will become smooth, creamy and slow to pour (2-3 minutes).

Immediately remove from heat and pour custard through a strainer into bowl.

Add vanilla extract, mixing thoroughly into the strained custard.

Refrigerate in airtight covered container until ready to serve.

Tip:
- You can prepare this cream 1 day in advance.

- Add 1 tsp. cornstarch to the sugar mixture to avoid any problem such as clumping while cooking the cream.

Crème Patissière
Cream Puff Pastry Filling

This creamy filling is a staple in French pastries. It's easy to make and serves as a lovely topping for fresh berries and fruits. Flavor with vanilla, chocolate or coffee as a pastry filling for éclairs or cream puffs.

Serves: 6
Prep.: 20 min. Cook.: 3 min.

- 2 cups whole (1/2 liter) milk
- 4 egg yolks
- 1/2 cup (60 grams) flour or gluten-free flour or corn flour
- 1/2 cup (100 grams) granulated sugar
- 2 tsp. vanilla extract or 2 Tbsp cocoa powder for chocolate flavoring or 2 tsp. espresso powder for coffee flavoring

Pour milk into a small saucepan. Add either vanilla extract, chocolate powder or espresso powder.

Cook, stirring occasionally until hot (do not allow to boil). Remove saucepan from heat.

Whisk egg yolks, flour and sugar in a heatproof bowl until well combined. Pour hot milk mixture over egg yolk mixture, whisking briskly.

Return mixture to saucepan over medium heat. Cook at a gentle heat, stirring constantly to prevent burning. When the mixture comes to a boil and thickens, remove from the heat.

Tip:
- Serve custard warm or cold over fresh or stewed fruit.

- Use as filling for cream puffs or éclairs. (page 38)

- Can be refrigerated up to 2 days.

Crème Chantilly
Whipped Cream

What a difference between real whipped cream and that stuff in the spray can! Easy to prepare, a dollop of Crème Chantilly will provide a voila to your grand finale dessert.

Serves: 6
Prep.: 10 min.

- 1 cup (237ml) cold whipping cream
- 1/3 cup (35 grams) confectioners (powdered) sugar
- 1 tsp vanilla extract

Chill heavy mixing bowl in freezer, about 15 minutes.

Remove bowl from freezer; add cream, sugar and vanilla. Using electric mixer, beat on high speed until stiff peaks form, about 2 minutes.

Serve immediately.

Tip:
An essential for enhancing any dessert.

Acknowledgments

From Yolande

To my dear friend Lisa who had the idea of this book. Our more than 15-year friendship has sustained us through our evolving vision, concept and creation of this cookbook.

Thank you to my dear Lucie and her friend Clémentine, university students in design. Lucie spent days designing this cookbook, sharing her talent and love. Lucie's contribution provided a multigenerational perspective.

Thank you to my friend Linda who spent many hours with me proofreading the recipes.

Mille mercis Jessica who polished the editing with talent!

Merci to my husband, Jean-Claude, for 47 years of happy and harmonious marriage. Your work took us to Germany, Singapore, the United States and China. Living in different cultures has enhanced our lives. Jean-Claude, you too are a cook and you make the best ratatouille I've ever eaten! We are proud of our two sons, Frédéric and Laurent who love cooking and are devoted to their families.

From Lisa

To our mutual friend, Christine Page, merci mille fois for your assistance. As a French-speaking American chef, your eye for detail clarified the recipes in this book.

Thank you to my husband, John. Your patience and support throughout our 44 years of marriage has been heroic, including cheerfully consuming Hamburger Helper as newlyweds.

Love always to our sons, Erik and Alex.

To dear friends and family, near and far, thank you.

Lisa Dane, Editor & Yolande Favreau Author/ Chef de Cuisine

Author Yolande Favreau cooking with her granddaughters Lucie and Nina

Author and Chef Yolande Favreau organizes quarterly pastry workshops for *Welcome to France,* an association of diplomats in Paris connected with the Ministry of Foreign Affairs.

Yolande teaches pastry workshops for members of *AVF, Home of French Cities* welcome organization and *Bagatelle Friendship*, located in Neuilly-sur-Seine.

Yolande's culinary training includes classes at the Ritz Escoffier in Paris. Her professional friends include Chef Muriel Béal, who graduated from the prestigious Ferrandi School of Culinary Arts. Yolande and Muriel teach pastry-making together to classes and small groups.

Editor and Writer Lisa Dane is content editor and feature writer for the publication, "Behind the Gates." Her company, DANE & Associates, includes writing, editing and marketing services.

Several of Dane's projects include editing and book launch for the romantic suspense novel, *The Dordogne Deception*, content editing for national best-selling mystery writer Cindy Sample (*Dying for a Date Series*), and Content Editor for YA fiction, *Noni's Little Problem*, set in Depression-era Missouri.

Find DANE & Associates on Facebook:
https://www.facebook.com/daneandassociates

Find Yolande Favreau on Instagram
https://www.instagram.com/yolandefavreau3

Contact: yolande.lisabook@gmail.com

Find us on Facebook and Instagram
Simple.Delicious.And Very French

Made in the USA
Columbia, SC
12 October 2018